THE PALEO INSTANT POT COOKBOOK

FOR RAPID WEIGHT LOSS AND A HEALTHIER LIFESTYLE

Amazing, easy and delicious Paleo diet recipes under 30 mintutes.

How to avoid the top 8 mistakes on Paleo diet

MEGAN MILES

Table of Contents

Description:

The Paleo diet (the shortened name for the Paleolithic diet) is regarded as one of the healthiest dietary strategies since this nutritional approach is fully compatible with your body's genetics, helping you stay strong, lean and energetic.

Within this book, you will be able to gain access to stunning tips and delicious *Paleo recipes for rapid weight loss* to help you achieve well-being, happiness, and beauty without boring workout sessions. What's more, this book **contains secrets that have never been released** about the Paleo diet protocols.

WHY WILL YOU BUY THIS BOOK INSTEAD OF ANOTHER?

- **Secret tips for successful weight loss on a Paleo diet such as**: how people can suppress their hunger when following a specific diet, and how to keep motivated to take up the *Paleo diet for rapid weight loss* without stopping in the middle…
- **Every recipe provides detailed information regarding its nutritional components, along with the number of calories**. Hence, you will be able to adjust your diet to maximize the outcomes of these Paleo recipes
- All recipes that can be prepared easily and **quickly under 30 minutes:** Breakfast, lunch and dinner, dessert and snack recipes (under 30 minutes)

- You can find out information about Paleo diet and Instant Pot in tabular form, **image of the dish for each recipe. You can't find duplicate recipe**
- And of course, much, much more!

Those who needs this book:

- Those who want to stay healthy and become more beautiful

- Those who want to achieve well-being and happiness

- Those who want to improve their Paleo diet effectively

- Those who are trying to gain a slimmer figure and lose weight in a completely safe and natural way

This book provides information on the following:

- Fundamental knowledge on the Paleo diet, including its protocols, and its positive impacts for human beings' health
- How instant pots help you during the process of taking up the Paleo diet, along with overall explanations of instant pot models and functionalities
- The hidden connection between Paleolithic recipes with an instant pot
- Simple and delicious *Paleo instant pot recipes* for homemade meals
- Top 8 popular mistakes Paleo dieters usually make, so you can avoid encountering these issues

CHAPTER I. INTRODUCTION

Do you hate yourself for constantly gaining weight, and have no idea how to stop that nightmare from going on? Are you looking for a potent method to start cutting down on your extra weight without damaging your health? Or have you just simply heard about the famous Paleolithic Diet, and you want to switch to this eating strategy to look for a healthier life?

If your answer is yes to one of the above questions, you are not alone. The majority of those who are currently not satisfied with their life is significantly due to their non-strategic dietary habits. And if you want to change that, you must know that it is difficult. Nothing is impossible, and I'm going to present an A-to-Z guideline that leads you through the detailed understanding of the Paleo Diet, what it involves and how it can help you.

CHAPTER II. OVERVIEW

1. What is the Paleo Diet?

As a matter of fact, the Paleo Diet (the shortened name for the Paleolithic Diet) is regarded as one of the healthiest dietary strategies since this nutritional approach is fully compatible with your body's genetics, helping you stay strong, lean and energetic.

Much research has been conducted in biochemistry, dermatology, ophthalmology, biology and other different disciplines, and it has been pointed out that our modern eating habits consist of excessive amounts of sugar, trans fats, and refined foods. These elements can lead to degenerative diseases like cancer, heart conditions, Alzheimer's, obesity and infertility.

a) Origins

Adrienne Rose Johnson states that the belief that a specific type of ancient diet has superior features to modern eating habits first appeared in the 1890s. Dr. Densmore, one of the supporters of the idea, affirmed that bread is one of the causes of death, whereas Dr. John Harvey Kellogg proclaimed that a diet containing grain-based and starchy ingredients was extremely beneficial.

The Paleolithic Diet ended up being listed as one of the most trending dietary plans in 2012 as the majority of well-known diet books written in this year were mostly based on this trend.

b) Health Benefits of a Paleo Diet

Healthy Cells

In case you do not know, every single cell located inside your body is composed of both unsaturated and saturated fat. To function properly and constantly exchange signals between the internal and external environments, your cells need to maintain a balance of these two fats.

On the other hand, the Paleolithic eating strategy has been scientifically proven to supply your body with a flawless balance as this diet promotes healthy amounts of both fats, whereas others restrict the consumption of one of them.

Maintain a Healthy Blood Glucose Level

Since the Paleo Diet limits the usage of refined sugar, you will find it easier to cross out spikes within your blood sugar, as well as bypass the feelings of exhaustion which were caused by sugar crashes. Nevertheless, if you are diagnosed with diabetes, it is suggested that you consult your personal doctor before taking up this diet.

Leaner Muscles

The Paleolithic Diet is based on meat as the primary ingredient, so you will be able to feed your muscles a sufficient amount of protein. As a result, this leads to a slenderer physique, and it also stimulates the growth of muscles if you practice weightlifting. A leaner form allows you to manage modern life's challenges more efficiently, especially with all the stresses happening in this digital era.

Avoid Gluten and Wheat

Because this dietary plan requires you to eliminate wheat products, which contains gluten, you will automatically follow a healthy diet totally free of gluten simultaneously. Scientific evidence has proven that gluten is one of the major reasons behind sluggish digestion and larger midsections, so cutting out gluten-based foods lets you improve your general health in a short amount of time.

Disease Prevention

Taking up the Paleo Diet means that you are reducing the majority of inflammatory foods you eat while consuming more foods that have a reverse effect, along with foods that include phytonutrients and antioxidants. These nutrients can fight off heart-related diseases and cancer.

c) The Principles of a Paleo Diet

Here is a list of the general principles one should follow when they decide to start the Paleolithic diet:

- Opt for real, homemade and well-prepared foods instead of the harmful junk foods exhibited in restaurants and convenience stores.
- Avoid eating corn, grains, rice and wheat, but if you want to eat some grains, try to prepare them in a sparing way to cut out toxins by soaking or sprouting. Rice is considered as the least harmful grain of all kinds, whereas wheat is always suggested to be eliminated. In fact, whole grains are as bad as refined grains.
- Eliminate sweets in your eating habits, such as corn syrup, honey, artificial sweeteners, sugar, agave nectar,

maple syrup and so on. You can try stevia if you really want to add sweetener to a dish.

- Stay away from modern oils made from seeds and grains like corn oil, soy oil or canola oil. It is much better if you make your own salad dressing and mayonnaise. Restaurants' fried foods should also be blacklisted, instead you ought to use vegetable oils for fried dishes.

- Say no to hydrogenated fats because they contain artificial trans fats. Opt for animal fats instead, such as ghee, tallow, lard and butter, along with unrefined olive oil and coconut oil.

- Beans and other types of legumes should also be crossed off from your diet, but if you want to have some legumes, eat them in a sparing way by soaking them.

- When it comes to workouts, do not focus on cardio sessions. Instead, you should opt for exercises which are highly intense within a short amount of time, such as sprinting, barefoot running or weight training.

- Vegetables are always a good option, but not the only choice. Their positive effects are multiplied when soaked in healthy fats. However, you should be careful of some vegetables' goitrogenic effects, especially when you decide to eat them raw.

Additionally, here is the list of what you can eat and what you must avoid:

Food Group	Eat	Avoid	Net Carbs	Recommended Maximum Consumed Amount
Meats	Bison, Turkey, Wild-caught fish, Beef, Chicken, Boar, Game meats	Factory-farmed meats	1.0	80 grams/serving
Grains	None	Rice, Quinoa, Wheat, Millet	25.8	200 grams/serving
Legumes	String beans, Snap peas, Haricot vert	Edamame / Soy and Peanuts	0.6	50 grams/serving
Vegetables	Brussels sprouts, Leafy greens, Cucumber, Squash, Sweet potatoes, Asparagus, Cabbage, Cauliflower	Nightshad, Tomatoe, White Potatoes, Eggplant, Onion, Goji Berries	2.6	200 grams/serving
Fruit	All fruits	None	1.7	175 grams/serving
Dairy	Coconut milk	Yogurt, Butter,	1.2	30 grams/serving

		Cheese, Ice cream		
Eggs	All eggs	None	1.4	150 grams/serving
Seeds and Nuts	None	Almonds, Coffee cashews, Sunflower seeds, Chia seeds, Pumpkin seeds, Sesame seeds, Macadamia, Cocoa	9.05	40 grams/serving
Fermented Foods	Sauerkrau, Kefir, Kombucha, Kimchi	Foods made from fermented soy	2	200 grams/serving
Sugar and alternatives	None	All sugars	12.6	10 grams/serving
Fats	Avocado oil, Lard, Olive oil	Butter, Margarines	3.2	50 grams/serving

d) Modern Day's Context and Feasible Solutions

Have you found yourself in the situation in which you think about fried foods on a regular basis? Do you eat more than you should? And do you end up feeling bad about yourself? Here are some tips for you to keep going with your efforts.

First of all, you need to point out to yourself that it is not the end of the world to say buh-bye to your favorite foods just for a while. A few minutes of meditation twice a day can help you feel calmer and help control your cortisol levels, making you feel less stressed out. Another tip is to spend a few minutes before every meal to ask yourself whether the food in front of you is optimal or not, and what food you can substitute for healthful reasons.

Although the Paleo Diet is a credible approach for a better state of health and well-being, you need to follow the strategies strictly in order not to damage your health. This is because some initial Paleo Diet users may suffer from fatigue, shakiness, and lethargy when they start getting rid of grains, legumes and starches from their diet. Therefore, it is better if you consult your personal doctor before starting any new dietary habits in general.

As a matter of fact, one of the reasons why the Paleo Diet is so popular is because it is the safest way to cut down on weight. Initially, most Paleo users will witness a dramatic loss of between 5 to 10 pounds after the first week. Starting from the second week, however, the loss will become slower, signaling a period of steady weight loss.

Here is an important note that you need to keep in mind. According to scientists, it is recommended that you constantly follow the Paleo Diet even after you achieve your goals, not only due to its weight-loss effects, but also because of its positive impact to human being's health. Nevertheless, if you really need to stop, try inserting the Paleo protocols into your daily meals.

2. Instant Pot

a) What is an Instant Pot?

In the recent years, there is no doubt that people are fond of their slow cookers, blenders and cherish their food processors, but the popularity of instant pots – a brand-new household appliance – is constantly soaring. To be specific, an instant pot can be described as a combination of a slow cooker, yogurt maker, rice cooker and electric pressure cooker, and it even promotes a more convenient cooking experience.

What sets this trending generation of cookers apart from other predecessors is that it is equipped with a set of self-regulating safety characteristics, including specialized sensors which can monitor the device's amount of pressure and temperature. All you must do is plug it in, push the button and let it do its job.

b) Primary Instant Pot Models

In general, there is a total of four major models of the instant pots, and this ebook is going to list the four of them in the order in which they were created. To put it another way, compared to the previous model, every new model has similar functions as the preceding one with some additional features.

Basically, the most common point among all kinds of instant pots is that they have a cooking surface made of stainless steel with the same safety features.

LUX

The LUX model is a feature-packed multipurpose cooker which can slow cook, make rice, maintain warmth, sauté, steam and pressure cook. Specifically, the LUX model is one of the first generations of instant pots, so it is easy to understand why it is not equipped with the setting to cook at low pressure, and it can't make yogurt either.

DUO

This instant pot's model has been regarded as the most successful version so far. Particularly, the DUO model has similar features with the LUX model, plus it can also make yogurt. Besides, after receiving feedbacks from customers, manufacturers have added two more pressure settings (low and high). Also, there are some small slots on the handles, letting you hang the lid over the side to save space in your kitchen.

SMART app

The most updated instant pot model is the SMART app. As I have stated, this model has all the functions of the DUO and LUX models, and it is also equipped with an informative screen with large number buttons. Not to mention that it is connected with a mobile application via Bluetooth. This convenient application allows you to dictate the specific duration, pressure and temperatures of each recipe in particular sequences.

Due to the application's ease of use, you can handle exactly the temperature of the pot, as well as how long the cooking session lasts, and decide whether to proceed to the following temperature setting or stop the instant pot by utilizing "recipe scripts."

The SMART app model is also a unique choice in the market which can pressure cook regardless of sequences. In other words, you can set up a script for the instant pot to slow cook, pressure cook, then turn off and stay at the warm setting for how-ever long you want.

DUO PLUS

This model has been renowned for breaking the limits of the traditional instant pots.

Specifically, the DUO PLUS model is actually an upgraded version of its original edition – the DUO model, and it has similar functions as the DUO one, along with the extra "cake" and "egg" programs (pre-set pressures and times).

The display screen is also fixed and has a new interface that lets the cook find it easier to differentiate the pot's settings, such as pressure cooking, heating, keeping warm and so on. It also can record the most recent pressure setting and cooking time.

ULTRA

This model presents a brand-new interface compared to older instant pot versions with the addition of the spin dial, so the ULTRA model permits users to customize the settings based on their purposes. Not only does it allow you to decide the cooking duration (from 60 seconds to above 5 hours), the pressure level (low and high), as well as set the countdown timer.

c) Key Tips to Leverage Instant Pot Settings

An ordinary instant pot has a total of 16 different settings, which is the reason why it is said to look like a dashboard. Here is a detailed guide to help you harness the beneficial power of this household device. Particularly, it denotes the words appearing on each button, and how to customize the settings of the instant pots like an expert cook.

Every button illustrates a specific cooking type, and each button allows you to preset the cooking time so that you do not have to remember it by yourself. What's more, the information shown on the screen lets you identify the actual state of the pot.

The table below gives you a summary of what each button of the instant pot means, along with the suitable cooking time and pressure setting for each cooking type.

	Button	Pressure Level	Cooking Duration
1	Stew/Meat	High	35 minutes
2	Poultry	High	15 minutes
3	Multigrain	High	40 minutes
4	Steam	High	10 minutes[1]
5	Pressure	High or low	Manual[2]
6	Yogurt	3 programs	Manual[3]
7	Manual	Adjustable (High as default)	Self-control using the +/- button
8	Cancel/Keep warm	N/A	Manual[4]
9	Soup	High	30 minutes
10	Chili/Bean	High	30 minutes
11	Rice	Low	Auto
12	Porridge	High	20 minutes
13	Slow cook	Normal	4 hours
14	Adjust	N/A	N/A
15	Sauté	Normal	Manual
16	Timer	N/A	Manual
[1]	rack is used to avoid burning		
[2]	suitable for making bone broth		
[3]	pasteurize milk, make yogurt or ferment rice		
[4]	automatically switch to this setting after the set time is over		

As indicated above, each function has a pre-set cooking time, so with recipes that require a specific number of minutes for cooking, opt for the "Manual" button. Specifically, press the "+" or "-" button to increase or decrease the cooking time as you wish.

In addition, the "Timer" function is specially designed for delayed cooking. To activate this mode, you must choose a particular cooking function, make suitable adjustments, and hit the "Timer" button while using the "+" or "-" button to set the cooking time.

In terms of the "Slow Cooker" mode, it is divided into 4 default slow-cook timings. What you need to do is press the button to choose the wanted temperature, which is low (190-201°F), normal (194-205°F) or high (199-210°F). Similarly, adjust the "+" and "-" button to customize the cooking time.

Besides, if you need to cook a specific dish at low or high pressure, you can easily switch between the two modes by hitting the "Pressure" button on the instant pot. Another special function is the "Sauté" mode, the one you use to pressure cook foods without the lid. To adjust the temperature, you need to press "Sauté" once or twice to choose the browning mode or simmer mode.

3. The Intimate Connection between Instant Pot and Paleo Diet

In this section, I am going to emphasize six essential reasons why you should utilize the instant pot to make your Paleolithic recipes.

- It reduces the time needed for preparations, especially the time it takes to make bone broth since you only need to spend a few hours making it using an instant pot instead of more than a day if you use traditional devices.

- It allows you to turn meat preparation into an easy job without a plan in advance. It is also possible for you to add additional cooking time, or cook meat which is frozen without thawing.

- You can pre-set your food to automatically cook and finish, then the instant pot will switch to the "keep warm" setting.

As a result, you will have a hot and ready delicious dish right after getting home from work for a maximum of 10 hours.

- The instant pots also serve as a slow cooker, which means that you can cross out some bulky appliances from your kitchen because it is literally a combination of several other devices.

- Instant pots have the feature to make coconut yogurt in a much quicker time than waiting for it to become edible using the original method.
- This device's features enable you to prepare enough food for an entire month to feed a baby in only a few hours. Besides, when it comes to cooking for your child, pressure-cooking is regarded as the best option because it retains more beneficial nutrients than roasting or boiling.

4. Instant Pot for Paleo Recipes: How to Maximize the Benefits

No matter whether you have been following the Paleo Diet for a while or you have just gotten started with the instant pot, here are some useful tips for you to maximize the benefits of this relationship.

Read the manual carefully

As I have stated, the physical appearance of an instant pot can be a little bit overwhelming with all the functions and buttons. Therefore, keeping the manual handy allows you to have more confidence when choosing which mode to use. Not to mention that you are able to keep track of the safety precautions of those Paleo recipes easily.

Pay attention to the total cooking time

A lot of Paleo recipes mainly focuses on promoting quick cooking time, but hardly mentions how long it needs to sustain or release the pressure at the last line of the recipe. Hence, remind yourself to avert your attention to those extra time intervals too.

Wisely choose recipes

Start with simple recipes with a view to getting accustomed to your instant pot, then move on to more complicated ones. As soon as you feel more comfortable using your pot, adventurous Paleo recipes will no longer be a challenge.

Zero minute rule

In fact, you can always adjust the timer to zero minute, which is a perfect timing for cooking vegetables quickly. In other words, you instant pot will sustain the pressure and turn off instantly.

Sautéing

It is recommended that you directly use the sauté function within the instant pot to avoid dirtying addition dishes. This is extremely useful when it comes to sautéing brown meat or vegetables before cooking.

CHAPTER III. INCREDIBLE PALEO RECIPES FOR INSTANT POTS

1. Breakfast Recipes

Recipe #1: Braised Kale and Carrots

- Prepare: 5 minutes

- Cook: 25 minutes

- Yield: 2 servings

- Paleo Diet Crab ratio: 20% fat, 60% protein, 20% carb

- Nutritional analysis: 235 calories/serving

Ingredients

- 10 ounces of chopped kale
- 1 tablespoon ghee or other type of fat
- 1 sliced medium-sized onion
- ½ cup of chicken broth
- 3 medium-sized carrots
- Ground pepper
- 5 garlic cloves
- Balsamic vinegar
- ¼ teaspoon of red pepper flakes
- Kosher salt

Instructions

a) Put the ghee into your instant pot, then press the "Sauté" button to melt it, then add in the onions and carrots and stop when the combination is softened.

b) Mix the garlic in, keep stirring until fragrant for about 30 seconds. Pour the chicken broth, along with the kale and some pepper and salt to taste. Do not forget to make sure that you leave about 1/3 space at the top of the pot.

c) Push the "Cancel/Keep Warm" button, then continue to press the button "Manual" and "-" until it reaches "5". Cover the lid, make sure that the valve is geared towards "Sealing" and let the instant pot do its job.

d) You can either leave the pressure to naturally drop for about 15 minutes or use the quick release mode and the steam will instantly flow out.

e) Remove the lid, season until it matches your taste. Splash on a little bit balsamic vinegar and red pepper flakes if you prefer heat.

Recipe #2: Cooker Bone Broth

- Prepare: 3 minutes

- Cook: 20 minutes

- Yield: 8 cups

- Paleo Diet Crab ratio: 10% fat, 50% protein, 40% carb

- Nutritional analysis: 179 calories/serving

Ingredients

- 2 halves of medium leeks
- 1 medium-sized carrot, cut into three pieces
- 2.5 pounds assorted bones
- 8 water cups
- 1 teaspoon of apple cider vinegar
- 2 tablespoons Red Boat fish sauce

Instructions

a) Mix the vegetables, bones, vinegar, fish sauce with water, then cover the lid and set it for high pressure.

b) Set the countdown timer for 20 minutes, but it is recommended that the broth will taste much better if you spend more time leaving it on.

c) After the timer rings, turn off the instant pot and let the pressure naturally release before straining the broth. Enjoy!

Recipe #3: "Lazy Devils" and Boiled Eggs

- Prepare: 3 minutes

- Cook: 16 minutes

- Yield: 8 eggs

- Paleo Diet Crab ratio: 40% protein, 40% carb and 20% fat

- Nutritional analysis: 150 calories/serving

Ingredients

- 8 large eggs
- 1 cup of water
- Toppings for these Lazy Devils (optional choices):
- Sliced radishes and guacamole
- Sliced Persian cucumbers, mayonnaise and Furikake

- Furikake, chipotle lime mayonnaise and sliced scallions
- Prosciutto, scallions, sliced cucumbers and chipotle lime mayonnaise

Instructions

a) Pour a cup of water into the steel insert of the instant pot, then put the steamer insert right inside and arrange 8 eggs carefully so that they make a single layer on top. Cover the lid and set the timer to 6 minutes with high pressure.

b) While the eggs are being cooked, fill in a big bowl with ice cubes and water.

c) When the timer goes off, grab the steamer's handles and put the eggs into the iced bowl. Leave it alone for at least 5 minutes.

d) After that, you can freely decorate these "Lazy Devils" in whatever way you want. Specifically, cut the eggs into halves and slather on your favorite toppings.

Recipe #4: Carnitas

- Prepare: 15 minutes

- Cook: 15 minutes

- Yield: 6 servings

- Paleo Diet Crab ratio: 60% protein, 30% fat, 10% carb

- Nutritional analysis: 314 calories/serving

Ingredients

- 3 pounds of boneless pork shoulder roast, cut into 2-inch cubes
- 2 teaspoons of kosher salt
- 2 teaspoons of ground cumin
- 1 teaspoon of red pepper flakes, crushed
- 1 teaspoon of dried oregano leaves, crushed
- 1 orange
- 6 peeled garlic cloves
- 1 quartered yellow onion
- 1 bay leaf
- 1 tablespoon of ghee, lard or avocado oil
- 1 diced onion
- 2 tablespoons of minced cilantro
- 1 head butter lettuce
- 2 sliced Hass avocados
- 1-2 sliced radishes
- 2 sliced jalapeño peppers
- 1 cup of salsa
- 3 quartered limes

Instructions

a) Place the pork in a big bowl and sprinkle it with cumin, oregano, red pepper flakes, and salt. After that, transfer the pork to your instant pot.

b) Peel the wide strips from the orange and add them to the pot, along with yellow onion, bay leaf and garlic. Separate the orange into two parts and make juice from them, then pour it into the mixture and keep stirring.

c) Hit the "Manual" button and set the timer to 35 minutes with high pressure and let it release naturally after you finish cooking. Uncover the lid, discard the onion, bay leaf and garlic. Adjust seasoning with salt to taste. Serve immediately!

Recipe #5: Steel Cut Oats

- Prepare: 4 minutes

- Cook: 17 minutes

- Yield: 2 - 3 servings

- Paleo Diet Crab ratio: 35% carb, 60% protein, 5% fat

- Nutritional analysis: 225 calories/serving

Ingredients:

- ½ cup of steel cut oats
- 2 cups of water
- 1 tablespoon of oil
- Salt

Instructions

a) Mix all ingredients in an instant pot, set the timer to 10 minutes with high pressure. After the alarm runs off, let the pot release pressure naturally. Stir the oats and wait until they absorb the water fully.

b) Top the dish with dried or fresh fruit, chopped granola or nuts, milk and your chosen sweetener such as maple syrup, agave syrup or white sugar.

Click to follow link to get free bonus:

http://bit.ly/2HViI6V

2. Lunch and Dinner Recipes

Recipe #1: Yankee Pot Roast

- Prepare: 10 minutes

- Cook: 20 minutes

- Yield: 6 servings

- Paleo Diet Crab ratio: 50% protein, 30% carb, 20% fat

- Nutritional analysis: 279 calories/serving

Ingredients

- 1 boneless beef chuck roast
- Kosher salt
- Ground black pepper
- 2 tablespoons of ghee

- 2 thinly sliced leeks
- 1 chopped celery stalk
- 1 chopped carrot
- 2 peeled and smashed garlic cloves
- 1 tablespoon of tomato paste
- ¼ cup of balsamic vinegar
- ½ ounce of rinsed porcini mushrooms
- 2 sprigs of fresh thyme
- 1 cup of chicken stock or bone broth
- 3 carrots, cut into 1-inch segments
- ¼ cup of chopped Italian parsley

Instructions

a) Season the roast with pepper and 2 tablespoons of kosher salt, then hit the "Sauté" button on your instant pot to melt off the ghee. After that, sear the beef until it turns brown on both sides. Transfer the beef to another platter.

b) Add the rest ghee, celery, carrots, salt and chopped leeks into the pot. Sauté the veggies until they become softened. Keep stirring for another 30 seconds after mixing in the tomato paste, garlic and vinegar.

c) Put the roast back into the instant pot, along with some thyme and porcini mushrooms. You also need to add the broth at this step. Cover the lid, then press the "Pressure Cook" or "Manual" button and set the timer to 75 minutes with high pressure.

d) Mix the carrot slices into the combination and continue to cook it for another 3 minutes with high pressure. After you finish, ladle the carrots and sauce on top of the pot roast with some Italian parsley as toppings. This dish tastes the best when it is served instantly with roasted veggies.

Recipe #2: Beef Stew

- Prepare: 10 minutes

- Cook: 20 minutes

- Yield: 4 servings

- Paleo Diet Crab ratio: 50% carb, 40% protein, 10% fat

- Nutritional analysis: 280 calories/serving

Ingredients

- 1 pound of quartered cremini mushrooms
- 2 tablespoons of tomato paste
- 6 smashed garlic cloves
- 2 tablespoons of coconut aminos
- 1 teaspoon of Red Boat fish sauce
- 2 thyme sprigs
- 1 bay leaf, dried
- Ground black pepper
- ¼ cup of chopped Italian parsley

Instructions

a) Toss the beef with kosher salt in a big bowl. Use the "Sauté" function to melt off your chosen cooking fat. Add kosher salt, mushrooms and onions. Keep sautéing until the onions become softened. Stir the garlic and tomato paste until fragrant.

b) Mix in the coconut aminos, thyme, fish sauce, bay leaf and salted beef. Stir until they combine. Use the "Keep Warm/Cancel" function of the instant pot and cover the lid.

After that, press the "Meat/Stew" button to activate the pressure cooker mode.

c) After you finish cooking, take out the bay leaf and thyme. Adjust seasoning with ground black pepper and salt. Serve with some Italian parsley.

Recipe #3: Thai Beef Stew

- Prepare: 10 minutes

- Cook: 25 minutes

- Yield: 8 servings

- Paleo Diet Crab ratio: 20% fat, 60% protein, 20% carb

- Nutritional analysis: 235 calories/serving

Ingredients

- 3 pounds of grass-fed beef brisket
- 2 teaspoons of kosher salt
- 1 tablespoon of coconut oil
- 2 tablespoons of Thai curry paste
- 1½ cup of coconut milk

- 2 tablespoons of coconut aminos
- 2 tablespoons of apple juice
- 1 tablespoon of Red Boat fish sauce
- 2 sweet potatoes, cut into big cubes
- 2 onions, chopped
- 2 big carrots, cut into 2-inch pieces
- Mixed herbs like scallions and cilantro

Instructions

a) Toss the beef with salt in a big bowl while using the "Sauté" button to prepare the coconut oil. As soon as the oil turns hot, pour in the curry paste and keep stirring until it turns fragrant.

b) Mix in the coconut aminos, fish sauce, apple juice and coconut milk. Stir until the sauce combines before adding the sweet potatoes, carrots, onions and beef cubes.

c) Press the "Meat" button and leave the instant pot on for at least 20 minutes with high pressure. After the pressure naturally releases, season it with fish sauce and salt and serve.

Recipe #4: Lemongrass and Coconut Chicken

- Prepare: 3 minutes

- Cook: 25 minutes

- Yield: 4 servings

- Paleo Diet Crab ratio: 60% fiber, 30% carb and 10% protein

- Nutritional analysis: 240 calories/serving

Ingredients

- 1 thick fresh lemongrass stalk
- 4 crushed garlic cloves
- 1 small peeled and chopped ginge
- 2 tablespoons of Red Boat fish sauce
- 3 tablespoons of coconut aminos

- 1 teaspoon of five spice powder
- 1 cup of coconut milk
- 10 drumsticks
- 1 teaspoon of kosher salt
- ½ teaspoon of ground black pepper
- 1 teaspoon of coconut oil and ghee
- 1 peeled and sliced onion
- ¼ cup of chopped fresh cilantro
- 1 lime's juice

Instructions

a) Peel, trim, then smash the lemongrass stalk. Mix the garlic, fish sauce, five-spice powder, ginger, and coconut aminos using a food processor or a blender. After that, add the coconut milk, and blitz until the mixture becomes smooth sauce.

b) Put the drumsticks within a big bowl, then season them with pepper and salt. Heat the insert up by using the "Sauté" function of the instant pot, then pour in a teaspoon of coconut oil or ghee.

c) After it melts, add the onions in and stir-fry them until they become translucent. Put the drumsticks in the pout and mix them with marinade above. Press the "Cancel/Warm" button while setting it up to the sealed position.

d) Use the "Pressure Cook" or "Manual" button to cook the combination for at least 15 minutes with high pressure. Once you finish, adjust the seasoning with salt, black pepper and some fish sauce. Enjoy your dish!

Recipe #5: Spaghetti Squash

- Prepare: 5 minutes

- Cook: 15 minutes

- Yield: 3 servings

- Paleo Diet Crab ratio: 70% carb, 10% fat and 20% protein

- Nutritional analysis: 370 calories/serving

Ingredients:

- 1 spaghetti squash
- 1 cup of water

Instructions

a) Cut the medium-sized spaghetti squash into two halves

crosswise, then use a big spoon to scoop the seeds in the squash's center out and remove the gunk.

b) Put the steamer trivet/insert within the instant pot and pour in one cup of water. Cover the lid and press the "Manual" button, and hold "-" to adjust it to 7.

c) After letting the pressure release, uncover the lid and tip the squash carefully to pour the collected liquid out. Use a fork to poke the squash to check whether the spaghetti is tender enough or not.

Recipe #6: Indian Curry Lamb Spare Ribs

- Prepare: 5 minutes

- Cook: 25 minutes

- Yield: 2-3 servings

- Paleo Diet Crab ratio: 30% carb, 60% protein, 10% fat

- Nutritional analysis: 183 calories/serving

Ingredients

- *For the lamb*

- 2.5 pounds of pastured lamb ribs

- 2 teaspoons of kosher salt

- 1 tablespoon of curry powder

- *For the sauce:*

- 1 tablespoon of coconut oil

- 1 chopped yellow onion

- ½ pound of ripe tomatoes

- 5 minced garlic cloves

- 1 tablespoon of curry powder

- 1 table spoon of kosher salt

- Lemon juice

- 1¼ cup of chopped cilantro

- 4 sliced scallions

Instructions

a) Season the lamb ribs with curry powder and salt. It is highly recommended that you use your bare hands to coat the spare ribs thoroughly.

b) Cover and put the ribs in the refrigerator for at least four hours.

c) When you are about to cook the ribs, use the instant pot to melt the coconut oil using the "Sauté" mode. After that, use the same mode to brown the ribs in two separate batches, then lay them in a plate when you finish.

d) Put the tomatoes and onion in a blender until smooth, whereas the ribs are still sizzling.

e) As soon as the ribs are already seared, add in some minced garlic to the pot, then quickly take off the pot from the head to prevent the garlic from being burned. This method promotes a yummy metallic taste to the dish.

f) Keep stirring the garlic until it gets fragrant for about half a minute before adding onion and tomato puree, then sprinkle some salt, lemon juice, curry powder and 1 cup of chopped cilantro and add the lamb in.

g) Remind yourself to carefully mix the spare ribs so that it is fully coated with the sauce.

f) Cover the lid of the instant pot and set the pressure to high level. After that, decrease the heat, so the high pressure is maintained for about 20 minutes.

g) Release the pressure naturally for at least 15 minutes, then adjust seasonings before the food matches your taste.

Recipe #7: Lamb Shanks

- Prepare: 3 minutes

- Cook: 30 minutes

- Yield: 4

- Paleo Diet Crab ratio: 40% carb, 57% protein, 3% fat

- Nutritional analysis: 330 calories/serving

Ingredients

- 3 pounds of lamb shanks
- Kosher salt
- Ground black pepper
- 2 tablespoons of ghee
- 2 chopped carrots
- 2 chopped celery stalks
- 1 chopped onion
- 1 tablespoon of tomato paste
- 3 garlic cloves
- 1 pound of ripe tomatoes
- 1 cup of bone broth
- 1 teaspoon of Red Boat Fish Sauce
- 1 tablespoon of balsamic vinegar
- ¼ cup of Italian parsley (minced, optional)

Instructions

a) Season the shanks with pepper and salt. After that, use the "Sauté" button of the instant pot to melt the ghee before searing the lamb shanks. Remove the shanks and lay them on a platter.

b) While preparing the lamb, chop the vegetables.

c) Lower to medium heat, then add in the remaining ghee, along with celery, onion, carrots with pepper and salt to taste. As soon as the vegetables become translucent, add garlic cloves, tomato paste and continue stirring for one more minute.

d) Put the lamb shanks back to the instant pot alongside with the tomatoes, then pour in fish sauce and bone broth with a little bit balsamic vinegar.

e) Grind some pepper before covering the lid. Press the "Cancel/Keep Warm" button to turn off the "Sauté" mode. Use the "Manual" button, pre-set the pot to cook for about 25 minutes at high pressure, and you are done!

f) After the shanks are thoroughly cooked, wait a little bit until for the pressure to drop. Plate the lamb and adjust seasonings. Sprinkle some fresh parsley over the hot dish and enjoy!

Click to follow link to get free bonus:

http://bit.ly/2HViI6V

Recipe #8: Grass Feb Beef Back Ribs

- No preparation needed

- Cook: 30 minutes

- Yield: 2 servings

- Paleo Diet Crab ratio: 40% carb, 50% protein, 10% fat

- Nutritional analysis: 205 calories/serving

Ingredients

- 1 grass-fed beef back ribs rack
- Dry rub
- Kosher salt
- ¾ cup of water
- 4 ounces unsweetened applesauce
- 2 tablespoons of coconut aminos
- 1 teaspoon of fish sauce

Instructions

a) Use a paper towel to dry off a back ribs rack, then sprinkle both sides carefully with kosher salt and dry rub. After that, wrap the ribs up to marinate in foil for about two hours before starting cooking.

b) When you are about to cook, remember to preheat a broiler and position the rack between 4 and 6 inches away from the heating source.

c) Take out the rack and cut it into pieces so that they would fit the instant pot. Lay the ribs on top of a wire rack in a baking sheet. Broil each side of the ribs for about 2 minutes to achieve a nice char. Add applesauce, fish sauce, coconut aminos, water to the pot, then stir carefully until the mixture combines and insert the rack into the pot.

d) Turn up the heating level. As soon as the instant pot achieves high pressure, turn down the heat again so that the pot can keeps its high pressure. Cook them under high pressure at least 20 minutes before leaving it alone to release pressure. Take the back ribs out of the pot and lay them on a wire rack in a baking sheet which is foil-lined.

e) Simmer the liquid until it is dried off to 2 cups, then eliminate the excess fat on top if you want and add more seasonings to your taste. Use the braising liquid to baste these racks, then continue broiling them for another minute before serving.

Recipe #9: Kalua Pigs

- Preparation: 5 minutes

- Cook: 30 minutes

- Yield: 8 servings

- Paleo Diet Crab ratio: 60% protein, 20% fat, 20% carb

- Nutritional analysis: 310 calories/serving

Ingredients

- 3 bacon slices
- 5 pounds of roasted pork shoulder
- 5 garlic cloves (peeled)
- Alaea Red Hawaiian Coarse Sea Salt (1½ tablespoon)
- 1 water cup

Instructions

a) Lay three bacon pieces on the surface of your instant pot's bottom, then push the button "Sauté" and it will begin sizzling after one minute.

b) Cut the roasted pork into three similar pieces. Use the garlic cloves if you want, then make some slits in every pork piece using a sharp knife, then tuck the garlic in.

c) Sprinkle the salt over the pork pieces evenly. While you are preparing the pork, the bacon is supposed to start sputtering within the pot. Remember to flip to other sides, then turn it off when the bacon turns brown. Lay the seasoned pork above the bacon while keeping the meat in one layer. Pour water in. Cover the lid.

d) Click the button "Manual", then press "+" until you pre-set the pot to 20 minutes in high pressure. Wait for it to finish. Put the finished pork into a big bowl. You can also sprinkle in a little bit of water or salt.

Recipe #10: Mexican Beef

- No preparation needed

- Cook: 30 minutes

- Yield: 4-6 servings

- Paleo Diet Crab ratio: 50% carb, 40% protein, 10% fat

- Nutritional analysis: 220 calories/serving

Ingredients

- 2½ pounds of boneless beef short ribs, beef chuck roast or beef brisket
- 1 tablespoon of chili powder
- 1½ teaspoon of kosher salt
- 1 tablespoon of ghee or other type of fat

- 1 sliced onion
- 1 tablespoon of tomato paste
- 6 peeled and smashed garlic cloves
- ½ cup of tomato salsa
- ½ cup of bone broth
- ½ teaspoon of Red Boat Fish Sauce
- Ground black pepper
- ½ cup of minced cilantro
- 2 sliced radishes

Instructions

a) Combine chili powder, salt and cubed beef within a large bowl. On the instant pot, push the button "Sauté" and add in the ghee to the mixture. As soon as the ghee has melted, add onions and sauté until the mixture gets translucent.

b) Keep stirring the garlic and tomato paste for at least 30 seconds until it turns fragrant.

c) Combine the seasoned beef with stock, fish sauce and salsa. Cover and lock the lid, then press the "Cancel/Keep Warm" button on the pot, then opt for the button "Meat/Stew" to proceed to the pressure-cooking state. If you cut your beef into smaller cubes, you can press "-" to decrease the pre-set cooking time.

d) After the stew is finished, the pot will automatically switch to the "Keep Warm" mode. Let the pressure naturally release for about 15 minutes.

e) Unlock the lid, then season with some pepper and salt to taste. This dish can be served instantly, or you can store in the fridge for maximum 4 days. Either way, reheat when you are ready to use, and sprinkle in some radishes and cilantro before eating.

Recipe #11: Mocha-Rubbed Pot Roast

- No preparations needed

- Cook: 30 minutes

- Yield: 4 servings

- Paleo Diet Crab ratio: 60% carb, 35% protein, 5% fat

- Nutritional analysis: 230 calories/serving

Ingredients

- For the mocha rub:

- 2 tablespoons of ground coffee
- 2 tablespoons of smoked paprika
- 1 tablespoon of black pepper
- 1 tablespoon of cocoa powder
- 1 teaspoon of Aleppo pepper
- 1 teaspoon of chili powder
- 1 teaspoon of ground ginger
- 1 teaspoon of sea salt

- For the roast:

- 2 pounds of beef chuck roast, then cut them into small-sized cubes
- 1 cup of brewed coffee
- 1 cup of bone broth or beef broth
- 1 small chopped onion
- 6 chopped dried figs
- 3 tablespoons of balsamic vinegar
- Kosher salt
- Ground black pepper

Instructions

a) Carefully mix the mocha rub's ingredients within a small-sized bowl. You do not need to use all the ingredients at this stage, so save a little bit in a tight container.

THE PALEO INSTANT POT COOKBOOK

b) Brew a cup of coffee, then put the beef cubes within a huge bowl before adding between three and four tablespoons of mocha rub. After that, toss in the bowl carefully so that the beef is thoroughly coated.

c) Combine the broth, figs, onion, balsamic vinegar and brewed coffee within a blender and blitz until the mixture gets liquefied.

d) Transfer the seasoned beef into the instant pot and pour the sauce above it, then turn it on and opt for the button "Meat/Stew" to activate its pressure-cooking mode. If your cubes have already been cut into small size, you can push the "-"-button to decrease the pre-set cooking time to a shorter duration. Leave the pot on and let it do its job.

e) After finishing cooking the stew, the instant pot will automatically switch to the "Keep Warm" mode. At this stage, turn it off and leave it alone to naturally release the pressure for at least 15 minutes.

f) Remove the lid. Check out whether the meat is tender enough or not. If not, do not hesitate to cook it with high pressure for another 5 minutes.

g) Put the cooked beef into a large dish and shred it using two forks. Adjust seasonings with pepper and salt until it matches your taste.

Recipe #12: Porcini and Tomato Beef Short Ribs

- Prepare: 5 minutes

- Cook: 26 minutes

- Yield: 4 servings

- Paleo Diet Crab ratio: 55% carb, 40% protein, 5% fat

- Nutritional analysis: 149 calories/serving

Ingredients

- 5 pounds of grass-fed beef ribs (short ones), then cut them into 3-inch pieces
- Kosher salt
- Ground pepper
- ½ ounce of porcini mushrooms

- 1 cup of boiling water
- 1 tablespoon of lard of other types of at
- 1 chopped onion
- 3 chopped carrots
- 2 chopped celery stalks
- 6 peeled and smashed garlic cloves
- 1 cup of marinara sauce
- ½ cup of bone broth
- 2 tablespoons of balsamic vinegar
- ¼ cup of Italian parsley

Instructions

a) Liberally season the beef ribs with pepper and salt. Put the porcini mushrooms within a large bowl, then pour boiling water in until they become softened.

b) Melt the lard using the instant pot with high heat. Sear the beef ribs in separate batches until they turn well-browned before transferring them to another platter.

c) Chop the vegetables, and toss the celery, carrots and onions into an empty pot. Turn down the heat to medium level, season with pepper and salt, then sauté until they turn soft.

d) Squeeze the liquid out from the softened mushrooms, then chop them up and put them in the pot with the garlic. Keep stirring the instant pot for about one minute before adding the broth, balsamic vinegar and marinara sauce inside.

e) Put the ribs back inside the pot, mix them carefully while turning up the heat to high level and wait for the combination to boil. Cover the lid.

f) As soon as the instant pot achieves high pressure, turn the heat lower and leave it one for a while. After that, take off the pot and let the pressure release naturally.

g) Add another tablespoon of balsamic vinegar and seasonings if you want until it fits your taste. Enjoy!

Recipe #13: Beef cooked with sauce

- Prepare: 5 minutes

- Cook: 20 minutes

- Yield: 6 servings

- Paleo Diet Crab ratio: 50% carb, 20% fat, 30% protein

- Nutritional analysis: 390 calories/serving

Ingredients

- ½ teaspoon of ghee
- 5 pounds of short ribs
- 1 peeled and diced yellow onion
- 1½ teaspoon of Madras curry powder
- 2½ teaspoons of fresh ginger
- 2 cups of diced tomatoes
- 3 tablespoons of Red Boat fish sauce
- 2 tablespoons of applesauce
- 1 trimmed stalk lemongrass
- 2 star anise
- 1 cup of bone broth
- 1 bay leaf
- 1 pound of peeled carrots, then chopped into several 1-inch pieces
- Kosher salt

Instructions

a) Press the "Sauté" button to melt off the ghee. Before searing, dry the ribs.

b) After you finish frying batches of beef, transfer them to a separate plate, then toss in some onions and continue sautéing until the combination turns translucent.

c) Add the ginger, diced tomatoes, applesauce, lemongrass stalks, curry powder, seared beef, fish sauce, bay leaf, and star anise. Pour the broth in, cover the lid and press the "Pressure Cook" or "Manual" button and set to 20 minutes of high pressure.

d) Let the pressure release naturally once you finish. Remove the lid and mix the carrots in. Cook for another 2-3 minutes with high pressure.

e) Adjust the seasonings with some more fish sauce and salt if you want. You're done!

Recipe #14: Salsa Chicken Tacos

- Prepare: 5 minutes

- Cook: 20 minutes

- Yield: 6 servings

- Paleo Diet Crab ratio: 75% protein, 10% fat, 15% carb

- Nutritional analysis: 276 calories/serving

Ingredients

- 2 pounds of skinless and boneless chicken thighs or breasts
- 1½ teaspoon of Potatoes Seasoning and Primal Palate Meat
- 1 cup of roasted tomato salsa
- Grain-free tortillas

Instructions

a) Season both sides of the chicken with salsa, then put them into the instant pot, cover the lid and press the "Pressure Cook" or "Manual" button and set it to 10 minutes for thighs or 7 minutes for breasts.

b) As soon as you finish cooking the chicken, transfer it to a big bowl and adjust the seasoning with pepper and salt to taste. Now it's all ready to dig in!

Recipe #15: Summer Italian Chicken

- Prepare: 5 minutes

- Cook: 25 minutes

- Yield: 6 servings

- Paleo Diet Crab ratio: 60% protein, 20% fat, 20% carb

- Nutritional analysis: 400 calories/serving

Ingredients

- 8 skinless boneless chicken thighs
- Kosher salt
- 1 tablespoon of ghee, olive oil or avocado oil
- 1 chopped onion
- 2 chopped carrots

- ½ pound of quartered cremini mushrooms
- 3 smashed garlic cloves
- 1 tablespoon of tomato paste
- 2 cups of cherry tomatoes
- ½ cup of pitted green olives
- ¼ teaspoon of black pepper
- ½ cup of fresh sliced basil leaves
- ¼ cup of chopped Italian parsley

Instructions

a) Sprinkle ¾ teaspoons of kosher salt over the chicken thighs. Use the "Sauté" function of the instant pot to melt the ghee. While it is shimmering, add the carrots, mushrooms, ½ teaspoon of kosher salt and onions.

b) Keep sautéing the veggies until they become softened, then mix the tomato paste and garlic and continue to cook for about half a minute.

c) Add the green olives, salted chicken and cherry tomatoes. Stir carefully.

d) Switch the instant pot from "Sauté" to "Pressure Cook" or "Manual" function. Remember to set the timer to 10 minutes for thighs or 7 minutes for breasts.

e) When you finish cooking, leave the instant pot on so that it can release the pressure naturally. After that, add some additional salt and black pepper if you want. This dish tastes the best when served instantly.

Recipe #16: Ground Beef Chili

- Prepare: 5 minutes

- Cook: 30 minutes

- Yield: 6 servings

- Paleo Diet Crab ratio: 70% protein, 10% fat, 20% carb

- Nutritional analysis: 180 calories/serving

Ingredients

- 1 tablespoon of ghee or avocado oil
- 1 diced yellow onion
- 1 diced red bell pepper
- Kosher salt
- 2 tablespoons of tomato paste
- 4 minced garlic cloves

- 2 pounds of ground beef
- 3 tablespoons of chili powder
- 1 tablespoon of dried oregano
- 1 tablespoon of ground cumin
- ¼ teaspoon of cayenne pepper
- 1 can of diced tomatoes, drained
- ½ cup of bone broth or chicken broth
- 2 teaspoons of fish sauce
- 1 tablespoon of apple cider vinegar

Optional toppings:

- Sliced avocado
- Slivered scallions
- Minced cilantro and diced white onions
- Coconut yogurt, unsweetened
- Lime wedges

Instructions

a) Heat up your chosen fat by hitting the "Sauté" button. When the oil shimmers, add bell peppers and onions with a little bit salt. Keep stirring while cooking until the veggies become softened.

b) Mix the minced garlic and tomato paste until the mixture turns fragrant. Add the ground beef and 1 teaspoon of kosher salt. Before breaking the meat up, brown it on both sides.

c) When the ground beef is not pink anymore, add the oregano, cayenne pepper, chili powder and cumin. Combine carefully so that it promotes the fragrant spices.

d) Toss the diced tomatoes, fish sauce and broth in, then cover the lid and press the "Pressure Cook" or "Manual" button while setting the timer to 15 minutes. When you finish cooking the chili, let the pressure release naturally before adjust seasoning with salt and apple cider vinegar. Use your favorite toppings to put on top and you're done!

Recipe #17: Lemon Olive Chicken

- Prepare: 2 minutes

- Cook: 10 minutes

- Yield: 3 servings

- Paleo Diet Crab ratio: 65% protein, 25% fat, 10% carb

- Nutritional analysis: 300 calories/serving

Ingredients

- 4 skinless boneless chicken breasts
- ½ teaspoon of organic cumin
- 1 teaspoon of sea salt
- ¼ teaspoon of black pepper
- ½ cup of butter
- Juice from one ½ lemon
- ½ thinly sliced lemon
- 1 cup of chicken bone broth
- 1 can of green olives
- ½ cup of sliced red onions

Instructions

a) Season the chicken breasts with black pepper, cumin and sea salt. Use the "Sauté" function to cook the breasts with butter until they turn brown on both sides.

b) Add the remaining ingredients into the pot, simmer the combination. Cover the lid and set the timer to 10 minutes. When you're done, let the pressure release naturally.

3. Dessert and Snack Recipes

Recipe #1: Hot Chocolate Fondue

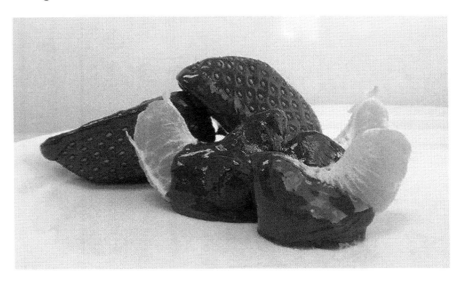

- Prepare: 1 minute

- Cook: 10 minutes

- Yield: 2-4 servings

- Paleo Diet Crab ratio: 50% carb, 40% fat, 10% protein

- Nutritional analysis: 480 calories/serving

Ingredients

- 3.5 ounce of bittersweet chocolate
- 3.5 ounce of fresh cream
- 1 teaspoon of sugar
- 1 teaspoon of Amaretto liquor

Instructions

a) Add two cups of water to the instant pot. In a separate heat-proof container, add large chunks of chocolate, along with some sugar, liquor and fresh cream. Put the container into the pot. Cover the lid and set the timer to 2 minutes under high pressure.

b) After you finish cooking, take the container out. Keep stirring the ramekin's contents vigorously for another minute until it becomes a thick and smooth mixture. Serve immediately with some bite-sized pieces of fresh fruit, bread cubes or cookies.

Recipe #2: Baked Apple

- Prepare: 5 minutes

- Cook: 20 minutes

- Yield: 6 servings

- Paleo Diet Crab ratio: 70% carb, 25% protein, 5% fat

- Nutritional analysis: 90 calories/serving

Ingredients

- 6 cored apples
- ¼ cup of raisins
- 1 cup of red wine
- ½ cup of raw demerara sugar
- 1 teaspoon of cinnamon powder

Instructions

a) Add the apples, wine, sugar, cinnamon powder and raisins into the instant pot. Cover the lid and set the timer to 10 minutes under high pressure.

b) After you finish, let the pressure release naturally. Take the apples out and serve in small bowls with cooking liquid.

Click to follow link to get free bonus:

http://bit.ly/2HViI6V

Recipe #3: Pot Beets

- Prepare: 5 minutes

- Cook: 15 minutes

- Yield: 4 servings

- Paleo Diet Crab ratio: 30% carb, 65% protein, 5% fat

- Nutritional analysis: 140 calories/serving

Ingredients

- 6 medium-sized trimmed beets
- 1 cup of water
- Kosher salt
- Ground black pepper
- Balsamic vinegar
- Olive oil

Instructions

a) Add one cup of water to the instant pot, then hit the "Manual" button and set the timer to 15 minutes with high pressure. After the beets are cooked, turn off the manual mode and let the pressure release naturally.

b) Remove the lid. Check whether the beets are tender enough by piercing a knife into them. If they are still too hard, turn the pot on and cook for another few minutes. After the beets cool off, cut the tops and skins off.

c) Slice the beets into pieces with similar size, then adjust the seasoning with pepper and salt, along with some balsamic vinegar and a little bit olive oil before serving.

Recipe #4: Korean Short Ribs

- Prepare: 10 minutes

- Cook: 25 minutes

- Yield: 6 servings

- Paleo Diet Crab ratio: 50% carb, 40% protein, 10% fat

- Nutritional analysis: 430 calories/serving

Ingredients

- 5 pounds of bone-in short ribs
- 1 tablespoon kosher salt
- ¼ teaspoon of ground black pepper
- ½ cup of coconut aminos
- 1 tablespoon of rice, coconut vinegar or while balsamic
- 2 teaspoons of Red Boat fish sauce
- 1 chopped Asian pear or Fuji apple
- 6 chopped cloves of garlic
- 3 chopped scallions
- 1 fresh ginger, cut into 2 pieces
- A handful of fresh cilantro

Instructions

a) Sprinkle the short ribs with pepper and salt, then transfer them to the instant pot. Add vinegar, apple or pear, scallions, ginger, garlic, fish sauce and coconut aminos in a food processor or blender. Blitz the combination until it turns smooth.

b) Pour the sauce on top of the ribs in the pot, then stir the combination carefully. Cover the lid, and set the instant pot's timer to 45 minutes by using the "Manual" function.

c) Naturally release the pressure, then open the lid and check whether you need to cook for another few minutes to make the ribs tender. If you have done this, put the ribs into a platter, and pour the liquid on top for seasoning, along with some pepper and salt. Serve with some cilantro.

Recipe #5: Pork and Napa Cabbage Soup

- Prepare: 10 minutes

- Cook: 20 minutes

- Yield: 6 servings

- Paleo Diet Crab ratio: 60% protein, 25% carb, 15% fat

- Nutritional analysis: 366 calories/serving

Ingredients

- 1 teaspoon of ghee
- 1 diced onion
- Kosher salt
- 1 pound of ground pork
- 6 thinly sliced shiitake mushrooms
- 2 minced garlic cloves
- 6 cups of bone broth
- 1 head of Napa cabbage, cut into 1-inch pieces crosswise
- 2 sliced carrots
- 1 big russet potato
- Ground black pepper
- 3 thinly sliced scallions

Instructions

a) Melt off the ghee by using the "Sauté" function of the instant pot, then add the diced onion along with a little bit salt when it becomes shimmered. Continue sautéing the onions until they turn soft.

b) Add the pork, sliced mushrooms and a little more salt. Cook the mushrooms and pork until the meat is not pink anymore, and the shiitakes turn tender.

c) Mix the minced garlic cloves in and cook for another 30 seconds until fragrant. After that, pour the broth in and turn up the heat to high level to the boiling point.

d) Add the potato, carrots and cabbage. Continue boiling the soup.

e) Turn down the heat to medium level. Remember to stir the soup occasionally until the fork can pierce the veggies easily. Adjust the seasoning with pepper and salt. The soup tastes better when it is garnished with scallions.

Recipe #6: Curried Cream of Broccoli Soup

- Prepare: 2 minutes

- Cook: 20 minutes

- Yield: 6 servings

- Paleo Diet Crab ratio: 70% carb, 20% protein, and 10% fat

- Nutritional analysis: 134 calories/serving

Ingredients

- 2 tablespoons of ghee, olive oil or coconut oil
- 3 trimmed and chopped leeks
- 2 chopped shallots
- 1 tablespoon of curry powder
- Kosher salt
- 1½ pound of chopped broccoli
- ¼ cup of diced apple
- 4 cups of chicken stock or bone broth
- Ground black pepper
- 1 cup of coconut milk
- Crisped Kalua pork
- Chives

Instructions

a) Melt off the ghee using the "Sauté" button of your instant pot, then add shallots, salt, curry powder and chopped leeks. Keep stirring until the alliums become softened and the curry turns fragrant.

b) Mix the apple and chopped broccoli in and mix them with the broth. Use the "Cancel/Keep Warm" function and set it to 5 minutes with high pressure. Cover the lid.

c) When you finish cooking the soup, turn off the pot and let it release pressure naturally. After that, use a blender to blitz the soup so that it becomes an aromatic smooth green purée.

d) Pour the coconut milk in, adjust seasonings with pepper and salt and serve immediately.

CHAPTER IV. EIGHT COMMON MISTAKES OF PALEO DIET USERS

1. Excessive Packaged Food Consumption

According to registered dietician Brooke Alpert, a nutritious founder, he concluded that foods which are labeled as Paleo-based, organic, or gluten-free may encourage you to buy them immediately because you think they are friendly with the weight loss process. The truth is that you can damage your health by savoring one more package of Paleo food.

In addition, a lot of Paleo-oriented products are rich in carbohydrates such as dried fruits, leading your body to retain more water, which is a very unwanted result for your weight-loss objectives. Therefore, next time you go to the supermarket, opt for fresh guac and vegetables, nuts, and berries instead of packs and packs of dairy-free, soy-free, grain-free snacks.

2. High-Level Protein Intake

As a matter of fact, you need to keep in mind that following a Paleolithic diet does not mean that you need to consume a huge amount of meat, and many Paleo diet users seem to have the same misunderstanding. Although protein is undoubtedly beneficial for your health since it allows you to strengthen your metabolism-revving muscle, your daily meals should not consist of over one-third of protein sources.

In addition, it is recommended that you opt for ideal protein sources such as fish, poultry and beef.

3. Lack of Vegetables

As one-third of the foods on your plate come from protein sources, it is highly recommended that half of it should be occupied with fruits and vegetables. This is because not only vegetables are low in calories, but they also help you take in a sufficient amount of fiber, enhancing your digestive system and suppress your need to find some snacks in the kitchen.

After filling half of your dish with greens, fill the rest of the space of your plate on healthy fats, including seeds, avocado and nuts. To efficiently promote the weight-loss effect of the Paleo diet, it is vital that you maintain a balance among satiating fiber, healthy fats and filling proteins.

4. Insufficient Lost Nutrients Compensation

Since the Paleo Diet requires you to cross out legumes, grains and dairy, you may end up missing some essential nutrients such as vitamin D, fiber and calcium. In fact, weight loss will not be effective or smart if you usually must deal with nutrient deficiency in the middle of the process.

Therefore, if you decide to take up the Paleo Diet, it is suggested that you consult a registered dietician with a view to making sure that your body consumes sufficient amounts of nutrients. Simultaneously, do not forget to eat more fresh vegetables and fruits every day so that you dedicate enough fiber to your diet.

Some ideal non-dairy calcium sources are cruciferous vegetables, including Brussel sprouts, broccoli and cauliflower, as well as leafy vegetables such as kale, spinach and collard greens. Additionally, increasing vitamin D intake via egg yolks and mushrooms is also a great option.

5. Portion Size Reduction

Before making sure that you divide every meal into decent amounts of nutrients on your dish, it is essential that you pay attention to your portion sizes in response to your Paleo diet. Even if you consume boatloads of vegetables and sufficient amounts of other food groups, it is possible that the weight-loss process might be slowed down, or you can even gain weight if you do not keep track of how much you are eating.

6. Arduous Self-Setting Rules

A key thing to remember is that popular dietary strategies are not always suitable for you and your body. If you are allergic or not intolerant with a diet that demands you to eliminate complete food groups, then you should not continue following it. Overall, try everything carefully with caution.

Even though most of your daily meals are based on the diet, you still must mix them with your individual food rules. For example, although taking up the Paleo Diet means that you must cut down on the amount of processed foods, alcohol and sugar consumption, while eating more fresh vegetables and lean protein. However, legumes, beans, whole grains and dairy should be kept at a sufficient level because that enables you to keep track of your healthy eating habits without feeling exhausted, leading to more long-lasting outcomes.

7. Loss of Calcium

Dairy is not the only food that provides your body with enough calcium. There are many calcium-rich alternatives which adhere to the Paleo strategies. It is suggested that you get a minimum amount of 600 mg of calcium every day by using whole foods. Full fat, grass-fed dairy is also a good choice because it is a healthy source of calcium if your body can put up with it.

8. Inadequate Attention for Other Lifestyle Factors

Many people have complained that the Paleo Diet does not help at all, while all they did is change their eating habits without going to bed early, eliminating coffee from their life, along with other bad lifestyle elements. Remember that not until you start paying more attention to sleeping enough and reducing cardio, as well as adding strength training, do you realize that the diet can be effective.

In conclusion, if you make up your mind to follow the Paleo journey, starting off with your food is a logical opening. Nevertheless, a popular mistake is to think that all your problems can be solved by alternating what is on your dish. In fact, true wellness and health is a multi-faceted issue. It is actually a synergy between different factors like renewing energy, building strength, nourishment and keeping a positive mindset.

CHAPTER V. CONCLUSION

To sum up, I hope that after reading this book, you will have a more general understanding of the Paleo protocols, as well as the intimate connection between Paleo recipes' potentials with a familiar household appliance – the instant pot. Besides, this book also points out the common issues you are likely to make when following this diet so that you can avoid making the same mistakes to maximize the beneficial outcomes of these above Paleo recipes.

ABOUT THE AUTHOR

My name is Megan Miles. I am a passionate recipe developer, a nutritionist and an author. My journey into eating Paleo started in 2013 after a year of unexpected weight gain, anxiety, and a slew of other issues affecting my overall well-being. The results of my new Paleo diet were so transformative that I began helping others find their own liberation through following a Paleo Diet and lifestyle.

I am passionate about healthy eating and sharing my knowledge with other people. I love food, and I believe sound nutrition is the basis for good health. And I am passionate about helping people improve their health! Over the coming months I am hoping to write a couple more books that will help people learn, start and succeed with certain diets.

Making the decision to change the way I was eating absolutely changed my life, for the better, and I look forward to helping you achieve the same, if not better results.

Made in the USA
Middletown, DE
06 September 2018